D1410979

Profiles

Bill Gates

An Unauthorized Biography

Sean Connolly

Heinemann Library
Des Plaines, Illinois

© 1999 Reed Educational & Professional Publishing.
Published by Heinemann Library, an imprint of Reed Educational & Professional
Publishing, 1350 East Touhy Avenue, Suite 240 West, Des Plaines, IL 60018

Designed by Visual Image
Printed in Hong Kong / China

03 02 01 00 99

10 9 8 7 6 5 4 3 2 1

Library of Congress Cataloging-in-Publication Data
Connolly, Sean, 1956-
    Bill Gates / Sean Connolly.
      p.   cm. -- (Heinemann profiles)
    Includes bibliographical references and index.
    Summary: A biography of the math whiz kid who grew up to co-found
Microsoft, the world's leading computer software firm.
    ISBN 1-57572-691-2 (lib. bdg.)
    1. Gates, Bill, 1955- --Juvenile literature. 2. Gates, Bill,
1955- . 3. Businesspeople--United States--Biography--Juvenile
literature. 4. Computer software industry--United States--Juvenile
literature. 5. Businessmen. [1. Gates, Bill, 1955-
2. Businessmen. 3. Computer software industry. 4. Microsoft
Corporation--History.] I. Title. II. Series.
HD9696.2.U62G373   1999
338.7'610053'092--dc21
    [B]   98-23409
                                                        CIP
                                                         AC

Acknowledgments
The Publishers would like to thank the following for permission to reproduce photographs:
AP pp. 46 (both), 47, 50; Camera Press: D Lomax p. 40, B Snyder p. 32; Corbis p. 22: Photoreporters p.
24; John Frost Newspaper Archives p. 38; IBM UK Ltd. p. 30; Phil Jensen, Burgermaster p. 35;
Lakeside School pp. 10, 12; Microsoft pp. 17, 18 (both), 21, 23, 25, 34, 43; National Motor Museum,
Beaulieu p. 41, Popperfoto pp. 4, 49 (upper), Stock Market: A Schein p. 39; Sygma: D Livingston pp.
44, 49 (lower), M Urban p. 49; Topham Picturepoint p. 8.

Cover photograph reproduced with permission of Universal Pictorial Press and Agency.
Every effort has been made to contact copyright holders of any material reproduced in this book.
Any omissions will be rectified in subsequent printings if notice is given to the Publisher.

Any words appearing in the text in bold, **like this,** are explained in the Glossary.

This is an unauthorized biography. The subject has not sponsored or endorsed this book.

CONTENTS

WHO IS BILL GATES? 4

CHILDHOOD 6

CONFRONTING A COMPUTER 10

THE BIRTH OF MICROSOFT 14

DROPOUT MAKES GOOD 18

WORLD EXPOSURE 22

THE PEOPLE WHO COUNT 24

ATTRACTING THE BEST 28

THE DEALS PAY OFF 30

LIFE AT MICROSOFT 34

BILLIONAIRE BILL 36

A WAVE OF TRIUMPHS 40

WINDOWS TO THE FUTURE 44

A VIEW ON GATES? 48

BILL GATES—TIMELINE 52

Glossary 54

Index 56

More Books to Read 56

WHO IS BILL GATES?

Imagine finding that your school has just gotten the best toy possible, and that you are allowed to play with it in your spare time. That would be a dream come true for many children. Imagine that you could keep playing with that toy when you grew up, and that it would help you become the richest person in the world.

These dreams have all come true for Bill Gates, who is the most famous person in the world of computers. At school he quickly unlocked the secrets of programming computers, and he used this skill to build Microsoft, the company that is now the leading maker of software for **personal computers** in the world.

Bill Gates has played a prominent role in publicizing Microsoft products.

DREAMS FOR THE FUTURE

Bill Gates set up Microsoft more than 20 years ago at the age of nineteen. Even then he could imagine a time when every home would have a computer, and his aim was to supply the products that would make these computers useful and fun.

Just what is a computer?

A computer is a machine that does calculations quickly. It "thinks" in binary language, which is made up of patterns of 0 and 1. It is a physical machine, made up of parts. The parts are called the hardware. In order for the machine to **process** the language it thinks in, it must have a **microprocessor**, usually a **silicon chip**. Any instructions or programs given to the computer are called software. The computer needs to have a language to act as a messenger between the person using it and its binary language. This special language is part of the software called the **operating system**.

Now nearly every home does have a computer. If you look further, you will see that the second part of Gates's prediction is also true. All the programs on your home computer probably rely on Microsoft software. So do the computers at your school or in your parents' offices. Even your favorite video games come with a Microsoft label.

MORE THAN LUCK

Bill Gates is a skillful and intelligent businessperson, and the huge success of Microsoft has made him a powerful person. Still, when people ask him about the secret of his success, he says it's luck. But it takes more than luck to take one young man from a small, stuffy room with a noisy computer to the headquarters of a company that employs more than 20,000 people in 56 countries. That something is the secret of Microsoft, and of Bill Gates.

A computer on every desk and in every home, running Microsoft software.
    Microsoft slogan since the late 1980s

CHILDHOOD

William Henry (Bill) Gates was born on October 28, 1955, in Seattle, Washington. His family was well known in the area, having been among the first settlers there in the 1800s.

SEEDS OF WEALTH

Bill's great-grandfather, also named William Henry Gates, had settled in the Seattle area in the 1880s when the port was beginning to grow rapidly. He made a fortune by building a number of businesses.

Bill's father, another William Henry Gates, grew up in a wealthy family and married Mary Maxwell in 1951. The Maxwells were also among Seattle's prominent families and had many links with the banking world.

Bill Gates poses for a family photo in 1971, with sisters Kirsty (left) and Libby.

A HAPPY CHILD

Bill was the second child born to the Gates family, coming between two sisters, Kristi and Libby. Even as a child, he was always on the move, constantly swaying in the cradle as a baby and tottering on the rocking horse as a toddler. Grandmother Adelle, an avid bridge player, nicknamed Bill "Trey," a card player's name for "three," because Bill's birth certificate read "William Henry Gates III."

THE WORLD'S FAIR

In 1962 when Bill was seven, the Gates family visited the Seattle **World's Fair**. It was called Century 21 because it focused on the technology that would lead the world into the 21st century. Each pavilion showed a different aspect of technical achievement. One of the main attractions was the Freedom 7 space capsule, in which Alan Shepard had made the first U.S. space flight with a person aboard in 1961.

The exhibits that made the most lasting impression on Bill, however, were the ones that showed the power of computers. In those days computers were much bigger than today's versions, but even these impressed Bill.

LIVE WIRE AT SCHOOL

At school Bill soon got the reputation for being the brightest child, especially in mathematics and science. He would finish maths tests long before his

The towering space needle, built for the 1962 World's Fair, is still a Seattle landmark.

classmates and could fill many pages with detailed essays about scientific subjects. He was so far ahead of the rest of the class that he began to get bored and sometimes landed himself in trouble.

Bill's parents felt that their son needed some sort of outlet for his energies, so they encouraged him to join sports teams. However, his mind wandered just as much in the middle of a football or baseball game. Boy Scouts was better for Bill, particularly because the local troop did not insist on wearing the scout uniform.

But school remained a problem. Bill could, and did, get top grades whenever he felt like it, but he began to become embarrassed about being teased for always doing so well, so he would sometimes deliberately get lower grades. Would he ever live up to his obvious potential?

> My most vivid memory is of Bill playing the game Risk. You try to take over the world.
> Stanley Young, childhood friend of Bill Gates, 1994

> I want to get back to [multiplication and] division because last year I was the best and I like it very much.
> Bill Gates, age ten, in a school essay

A mover and a shaker

Bill Gates's constant swaying and rocking as a child seemed to be a way to release extra energy. Gates has never lost that habit, and still surprises business colleagues by swaying back and forth while thinking through a problem or jumping onto a desk from a standing position.

CONFRONTING A COMPUTER

Bill's parents decided to send him to an exclusive private school, the all-boys Lakeside School. Lakeside School was like a New England **prep school**. Bill Gates entered the Lakeside School in September 1967 at age eleven.

The first year was difficult. Bill found himself in a new environment, and not only because of the rigid rules and discipline. Lakeside students were as bright as he was and they were competitive about grades in a way that Bill had never encountered. Before Bill had to stop himself from getting A's in every subject. At Lakeside he began to get B's. His only A grade came in an advanced algebra class.

The new machine

Bill began to mix with other boys in a math-science group. These boys shared an interest in **technology** and mathematics. When Bill started his second year, he and his friends found a bulky new machine in a tiny office of the mathematics and science building. The forbidding machine was an ASR-33 Teletype, which combined a keyboard, printer, and **modem**.

The machine was noisy and slow, but it could read computer programs, which could be typed in using the keyboard and saved on paper tape. More often a program would be written on dozens of cards, which had to be fed onto the machine in the right order.

The machine at Lakeside could do nothing more than read or produce taped programs. Its modem, though, linked it by telephone to a real computer through a system known as **time sharing**.

I go around saying I taught him all he knows. It took him a week to pass [overtake] me.

Bill Dougall, Bill Gates's teacher at Lakeside School

TRIPLE–C

Bill and his friends were ecstatic. A real computer! Until then computers had seemed to be huge, expensive machines housed in places where only government officials or academics could go. The idea that they, mere students, could sit and run their own programs was almost unbelievable. Before long they were running advanced programs using the **BASIC** computer **language**.

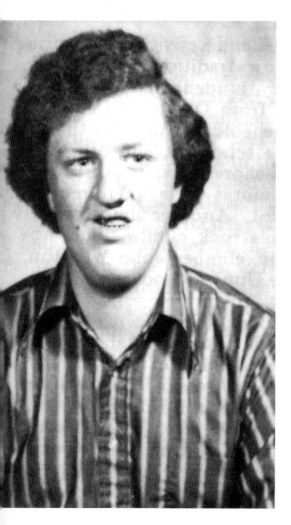

Gate's close friend and fellow computer lover, Kent Evans, is pictured shortly before his death in 1972.

Time sharing became too expensive for the school, but the Lakeside boys soon found another place to do their programming: the Computer Center Corporation in Seattle, also known as "Triple-C." Triple-C wanted to sell computer time to large businesses, but they needed to test their equipment. Who better to do this testing than the eager boys from Lakeside School?

FIRST BUSINESS DEAL

Bill, who was never very tidy, filled his bedroom with stacks of computer paper as he tried to work out programming problems. He would even sneak out of the house at night and take the bus to

Triple–C for more programming. Along with his Lakeside friends Paul Allen, Ric Weiland, and Kent Evans, Bill was becoming more ambitious. The young **programmers** began to see that there was money to be made while they were having all their programming fun. They called themselves the Lakeside Programmers Group, and in 1971 they wrote a program for a local business, Information Sciences, Inc. (ISI). The program calculated the weekly salaries of all the workers, including any allowances for tax, health insurance, and other deductions.

It was Bill's first business deal. They earned $5,000 of computer time, which they were able to use in creating and testing all sorts of programs they had written. Would there be more in the future?

Losing a friend

Bill Gates's closest friend at Lakeside School was Kent Evans, who was in the same year. Gates was devastated when he found out that Evans had died in a mountaineering accident on May 28, 1972. After an emotional funeral service at the Lakeside School chapel, Gates broke down in tears.

THE BIRTH OF MICROSOFT

Bill and his closest friends still concentrated on their computer projects in every moment of their free time. The Lakeside **Programmers** Group had had valuable use of powerful computers thanks to their successful deal with ISI. Their computing skills were increasing so quickly that by fall of 1972 they decided to build their own computer.

Paul Allen, who had already begun studying at Washington State University, told Bill about a magazine article on a new **microprocessor chip** that could become the brains of a new computer. Small and cheap chips like those in the article had already been used successfully in electronic calculators. The two of them bought one of these Intel 8008 chips and used it as the heart of a traffic-counting computer. They even set up a company, which they called Traf–O–**Data.** This project aimed to count the number of vehicles passing certain junctions and calculate the flow of traffic. With this knowledge of traffic flows, the police and other organizations could concentrate on the trouble spots. But Gates and his friends had done little research into how much they would need to spend to

The Lakeside Programmers Group developed a stylish letterhead for their new company, Traf-O-Data.

produce the program, and they did a poor job of trying to sell the idea.

Off to Harvard

Gates and Allen continued their research with Traf-O-Data, but the time came for Bill to think of college. His outstanding academic record gave him the choice of the best universities, and he chose to attend Harvard University, near Boston, Massachusetts.

Bill started at Harvard in September 1973. He went to a wide number of classes and did well even when he had little time to study. However, he did have time for late-night poker games, and he also managed to continue to help the Traf-O-Data project. At Harvard he became friends with Steve Ballmer, a lively student with a wide range of interests. Ballmer would be one of Gates's most loyal friends in later years.

Practical reading

Paul Allen had taken a job near Boston when he told Bill of yet another magazine article, about a build-it-yourself computer that used the powerful new Intel 8080 chip. It was called the Altair 8800 and is now recognized as the first real **personal computer**. From their difficult Traf-O-Data experience, Allen and Gates knew that developing the hardware of a computer was a slow process. Someone had already

21. Front-page news: the first issue of MITS *Computer Notes,* April 7, 1975.

ALTAIR BASIC - UP AND RUNNING

In January, when Popular Electronics featured the Altair Computer on its front cover, we knew that we had a great product. But no one could have predicted the enormous flood of inquiries and phone calls and orders that started hitting us about mid-January.

Partly because the Altair has generated such a huge volume of business, we have been able to speed up our Altair development program and broaden our horizons somewhat. Undoubtedly the most newsworthy of these developments is the introduction of a BASIC programming language for the Altair Computer.

That's right. We've got BASIC and it's up and running!

People who are familiar with programming and BASIC language will most likely understand why we're making such a big deal out of this. For those who aren't familiar, we offer the following explanation.

A few years back, realizing that computers needn't be so darn complicated, a group of professors at Dartmouth College developed a revolutionary, new computer language called BASIC language. This language was designed so that people with little or no computer knowledge could learn how to program.

BASIC language works because it is just what it says--it is, namely, BASIC. For example, when you want to instruct the computer to

PRINT something and you are using BASIC language, you simply type the word PRINT on your terminal or teletype keyboard followed by whatever it is you want the computer to print. BASIC is BASIC. It is simple and understandable.

To illustrate this further, let's take a look at this sample BASIC program, designed to calculate a simple interest problem.

```
SCRATCH ↵

10 LET P=650 ↵

20 LET T=18 ↵

30 LET R=.065 ↵

40 LET I=P*T*R/12 ↵

50 LET P1=P+I ↵

60 LET M=P1/T ↵

70 PRINT "TOTAL INTEREST IS";I ↵

80 PRINT "TOTAL MONEY OWED IS";P1 ↵

90 PRINT "MONTHLY PAYMENTS ARE";M ↵

RUN ↵
```

COMPUTER NOTES

APRIL 7, 1975

© MITS, INC. 1975

A PUBLICATION OF THE ALTAIR USERS GROUP   VOLUME ONE ISSUE ONE

MITS proudly announced the arrival of the Gates and Allen BASIC software in an April 1975 newsletter.

done it with the Altair 8800, but had the inventors found a form of the **BASIC language** that would make the computer actually work? Luckily for Gates and Allen, there was no such language.

SENDING OUT FEELERS

The company that developed the Altair 8800 was called MITS, and it was based in Albuquerque, New Mexico. MITS was selling thousands of its unbuilt Altair machines, even though buyers would soon learn that a machine could do very little without a language to make it work.

Gates and Allen, still working under the name Traf–O–Data, contacted MITS in early 1975. They promised to provide a form of BASIC software that

The first Microsoft advertisement appeared in *Digital Design* magazine in July 1976.

would work on the Altair computer. They worked day and night to produce their software before Allen visited MITS in March.

MICROSOFT IS BORN

The demonstration went almost like clockwork, and MITS agreed to take the software. MITS was so impressed that it hired Allen as vice president and director of software.

In April 1975, Gates and Allen reconsidered their position as partners in their company. Gates reminded Allen that while he was a paid employee of MITS, Gates had no other job. On that basis, they considered the partnership to be 60 percent for Gates and 40 percent for Allen. On April 5, 1975, they named their new company Microsoft. The name is made up from the words *micro*processing and *soft*ware.

Favorite reading

Gates has always been an avid reader. One of his favorite books at school was *Catcher in the Rye*, by J.D. Salinger. This novel is about a teenage boy who cannot stand to be surrounded by "frauds" and "phonies." Gates was inspired by the rebel hero, who sets out to find new ways to beat "the system." He saw his own programming efforts as a chance to beat large computing companies, the "System," in his view, at their own game.

DROPOUT MAKES GOOD

Microsoft had a name, a contract, and a staff. It continued to provide **BASIC** software for new versions of MITS computers, but each new deal made it easier for Microsoft to sell their product to other customers. Later in 1975, Microsoft hired its first paid employee, Marc McDonald, another former Lakeside student.

In 1976 Microsoft acquired its first real office, 1 Park Central Tower, Albuquerque and it hired Ric Weiland to take care of **bookkeeping** and legal matters and to act as a link with MITS. The two partners had other commitments, Allen to his MITS employers and Gates at Harvard.

Gates found it difficult dividing time between the computer center at Harvard (above) and Microsoft's offices in Albuquerque (right).

Good-by to Harvard

Gates continued a frantic mixture of poker playing, socializing, and last-minute studying when he was back at Harvard. It became obvious that Microsoft might not do as well if Gates kept flying between New Mexico and Harvard. In January 1977, in his third of four years at Harvard, Gates took the first semester exams and then flew home to New Mexico. He would never return to complete his degree.

Building the company

Paul Allen had left MITS in November 1976 and was working full-time for Microsoft when Gates returned in February 1977. The computer world was beginning to grow rapidly, and Microsoft was busy trying to write software that would tie in with each new advance. There were more employees, and they all seemed to be like Gates himself: young, male, and totally committed to computer programming. Working hours were long, and Gates expected everyone to work as hard as he did.

Gates and Allen were becoming well known, and they both knew that Microsoft would benefit from the articles they wrote for computer magazines and from public appearances.

New, larger contracts began rolling in, and by September 1977, Gates realized that Microsoft needed to be put in some sort of order. Microsoft's

General Manager Steve Wood hired Miriam Lubow as secretary and receptionist. She had never heard of software, and she was surprised to find that her boss, the company president Bill Gates, was only 21 years old.

BACK TO WASHINGTON

By 1978 Microsoft had managed to end its early contract with MITS, which meant that the company was free to chase other customers even harder. Apart from MITS, there were no possible customers in New Mexico, and Microsoft had to decide where to move their fast-growing company.

California, with its famous **Silicon Valley** of computer companies, was a possible choice for a move. Gates, however, had doubts about moving there. The first was that Microsoft employees might decide to leave if there were other companies at their doorstep. The other reason was that the sunny California weather might tempt employees to take days off for surfing or swimming.

Free Cokes

One of Bill Gates's first jobs for Miriam Lubow was to keep the company supplied with Coca-Cola. The first six-pack disappeared within minutes, so Gates told her to order it by the case. Eventually she ordered directly from the Coca-Cola company and started a tradition that continues even today at Microsoft: free soft drinks for all employees.

The Microsoft team (Gates bottom left) posed for a farewell photograph before leaving Albuquerque in 1978.

Gates decided that the obvious answer was to move back to his home state of Washington. It would be close enough to California to do business, but the damp climate would encourage hard work indoors.

December 1978 saw Microsoft finish its first million-dollar sales year, totalling $1,355,665. By January of 1979, the company had moved to the Seattle **suburb** of Bellevue, Washington.

> Microsoft expects a level of dedication from its employees higher than most companies. Therefore, if some deadline or discussion or interesting piece of work causes you to work extra time some week it just goes with the job.
> Bill Gates, in an early Microsoft memo

World Exposure

The new offices near Seattle were on the eighth floor of the Old National Bank building, and Gates had a corner office with a view of Lake Washington and the mountains beyond. The office had a couch, where he would take catnaps during his long working days.

Japanese Freedom

The new year, 1979, saw Microsoft's first big deals in Japan. Kazuhiko "Kay" Nishi, Microsoft's **agent** in the Far East, had begun attracting business for the young American company.

One of the most important of these contacts was with the Japanese computer giant Nippon Electric Company (NEC). Kazuya Watanabe, one of its **executives**, visited Microsoft in 1979 and worked out a creative deal. Microsoft would not only provide software for NEC computers (the area in which Microsoft was becoming famous), but it would actually advise the Japanese company about how the

computers themselves should be made. This type of freedom was unusual for Microsoft in its dealings with U.S. companies, and Gates would press for this freedom in some of his later deals.

Kay Nishi helped turn Microsoft into an international company willing to take risks.

A BITE OF THE APPLE

One of the business relationships that Gates was eager to boost was with Apple Computers. Apple was becoming one of the biggest names in the computer industry because it made software as well as stylish, easy-to-use computers. Apple was so successful that its staff began to run out of time to write software to match the advances of the machines themselves.

One day over lunch, Gates and Allen came up with a solution for the Apple problem. They created what would eventually be called the SoftCard. This was a plug-in board that would allow Apple computers to work with advanced computer **languages.**

THE PEOPLE WHO COUNT

A t the end of the 1970s, the names of Microsoft and Bill Gates kept coming up when high-level computer **executives** met. Microsoft was still a small company in comparison with Apple and other top-selling computer firms, but it was making startling progress. Much of this image was due to Bill Gates himself.

Although he was not the most lively public speaker, Gates had a way of winning people over with his quick intelligence and the ease with which he grasped new problems.

H. Ross Perot is a successful businessperson who gained millions of votes in his 1992 and 1996 attempts to become U.S. President.

THANKS, BUT NO THANKS

In August 1979, Gates visited the Dallas headquarters of Electronic Data Systems, the huge computer service company led by H. Ross Perot. Perot's aims were simple at that meeting: he was offering to buy Microsoft.

Perot provided software for large **mainframe** computers, and he thought that by buying Microsoft, he would be able to jump into the growing market for **microcomputers**.

In the end, the discussions got no farther than the money stage. Gates asked for $40 to 60 million, and Perot thought it was too high. He would soon think otherwise.

A FRIEND AT THE HELM

Gates was right to be confident about Microsoft's future. It was earning millions of dollars a year and sales were growing quickly. However, nearly every big decision had to be made by one person: Gates himself. And the financial records of this high-flying company? They were not kept on computer but written out in longhand.

At the age of 24, Bill Gates was a match for the more experienced H. Ross Perot.

Gates decided to hire his old friend from Harvard, Steve Ballmer, for the job of assistant to the president of Microsoft. For the first time, Gates had someone to whom he could hand over the finances, legal affairs, and personnel work of the growing company. Despite growing rapidly, the company tried to keep the sense of being a team. There were Friday night parties to give the staff the chance to relax and unwind. But Gates began to be a less common sight at these parties as his work kept him away. However, when he was able to join his staff, he entered into the spirit of things. Once he bodysurfed headfirst down the staircase, leaving a worker wondering, "My God, this is the president of the company?"

Big Blue

One of the companies that had noticed Microsoft's rapid rise was IBM, the world's leading computer company. IBM had the nickname "Big Blue" because its male workers wore blue suits. By 1980 it was developing its own **personal computer,** but the plan was falling behind schedule. Where could it turn to find some help at this crucial stage, when rival companies might release their versions first?

The answer seemed to be Microsoft, and on July 21, 1980, IBM's software chief Jack Sams telephoned Gates and insisted on a meeting the next day. Sams and his colleague Pat Harrington were impressed with Microsoft's offices and the list of nearly 100 hundred happy customers who had purchased versions of Microsoft's **BASIC** software.

In the following weeks it became clear that Microsoft was IBM's first choice for providing software for the planned IBM personal computer. By August there was a firm commitment by both companies to work together, and an official contract was signed on November 6.

FOUNDATION OF A FORTUNE

Always on the lookout for new ideas, Gates learned of an **operating system** made by another local firm, Seattle Computer Products. The system was known as Q–DOS (Quick and Dirty Operating System). It would be able to arrange the many **applications** in a personal computer, and would be a valuable addition to the IBM deal. Microsoft signed a deal to **license** Q–DOS; on July 27, 1981, Microsoft bought a later version, 86–DOS, outright.

That purchase, for a total of $75,000, would prove to be an important step toward Microsoft's world dominance and the Gates fortune.

Pushing his own ideas

The freedom that Microsoft had enjoyed in its early experience with NEC allowed Gates to press for more of his ideas to be included in the planned IBM computer. Although it was more used to giving orders to its partners, IBM found itself listening to the bright young man, whose company might get them out of a tight squeeze.

Attracting the Best

Microsoft's growing fame meant that Gates and Allen had many visitors who came to try their ideas out on the high-flying company. One of these was a young Hungarian, Charles Simonyi, who came to the office just a few weeks after the IBM deal was signed. Simonyi had grown up under Hungary's **communist** rule, and had learned his computer skills on very basic Russian machines. When he arrived in the United States as a teenager, he found it easy to come up with creative solutions to basic computer problems.

New directions

Simonyi had developed a number of ideas during the 1970s, including a **word processor** that used an early version of a **mouse**. When he arrived to demonstrate some of his work at the Microsoft offices in the fall of 1980, Gates was immediately impressed. Here was someone who could add yet more to the work being done on the IBM project. Within weeks Simonyi became Microsoft's director of advanced product development.

Incorporating success

By mid-1981, after just six years, the world was beginning to see the importance of Microsoft, and its two founders, Gates and Allen, were becoming celebrities. The June 1981 issue of the business magazine *Fortune* featured the pair in an article about leading figures in the computer industry.

There was good reason to single out Microsoft. Under Ballmer's business guidance, the company kept growing at an astonishing rate. It became a Washington State **corporation** on July 1, 1981, with **stock** divided among the leading people in the company. Gates got 53 percent, Allen got 31 per cent, Ballmer got 8 percent and several others got slightly smaller portions. Gates got the largest proportion because he was taking more of a risk, having dropped out of school, while Allen had been on the staff at MITS.

Basic Strategy: The IBM Strategy. Don't be the first to introduce a new technology. Be second, and make more money on it.

Microsoft consultant Paul Heckel, May 1980

THE DEALS PAY OFF

B y the beginning of 1981, Bill Gates had positioned Microsoft to be in an excellent position in the computer world. The IBM contract, and the freedom that it gave Microsoft, was a potential fortune maker in itself. Just as important, however, was the way in which Gates had gone about taking control of the DOS **operating system**.

VISION OF THE FUTURE

Although Gates cannot be credited with developing DOS, he was one of the first people in the world to grasp its importance. Gates knew that the world of

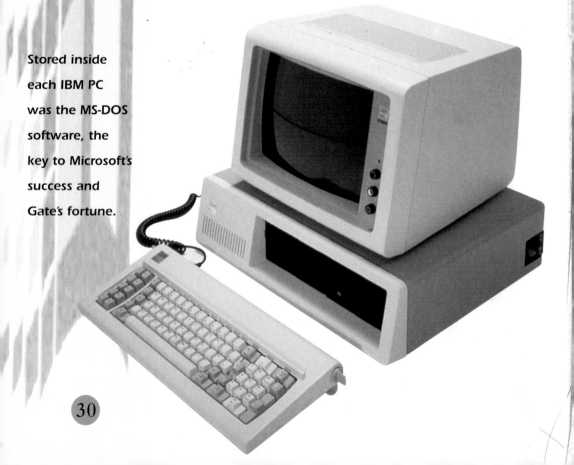

Stored inside each IBM PC was the MS-DOS software, the key to Microsoft's success and Gate's fortune.

the **personal computer** was about to be blown wide open, and that the idea that there could be a computer in every household was soon to be a reality. Each of these millions of computers would need an operating system, and Gates was determined that DOS—now called MS-DOS because of Microsoft ownership—would be that system.

"A COMPUTER ON EVERY DESK"

IBM knew that DOS was the ace up Gates's sleeve, and its designers were desperately trying to produce an operating system of their own. But their own deadline for the launch of the IBM PC was soon approaching, and it looked as though Gates and the Microsoft team would win that important race.

On August 12, 1981, IBM announced the launch of its new personal computer. Some experts in the computer world considered it to be a slow machine with not much in its favor. Others, however, knew that this new PC was likely to be a top seller, if only because of the enormous power that IBM had in its marketing, advertising, and sales force. The *New York Times* echoed the view of many people when it ran a story about the launch under the headline "A Computer on Every Desk."

HOW MICROSOFT WOULD WIN

The operating system behind this new world-beating PC was none other than MS-DOS, and Microsoft

Steve Jobs, the head of Apple Computers, realized that the future of Apple would be linked to Microsoft—and to Gates himself.

was ready to earn fat **commissions** on each personal computer that was sold. Gates predicted that 200,000 would be sold in 1982 and that the number would increase each year. He also knew that the PC had the potential to hold increasing amounts of memory, and that therefore it would be able to run new Microsoft software products in the future. By buying an IBM PC, a customer would really be **subscribing** to Microsoft and its widening range of products.

> I think five years from now the amount of software and the quality of software on this machine will be incredible. It will dwarf what is available on **mainframes, minicomputers, and other machines.**
>
> Bill Gates on the IBM PC, 1982

Just as important though, the IBM contract gave Microsoft the right to sell other versions of DOS to other manufacturers. Another company could build a computer that virtually mirrored the IBM PC, and IBM would not get a penny. But in order to run that computer, the manufacturer would have to use DOS —and Microsoft would have to be paid.

THE APPLE REACTION

The people at Apple computers felt that the IBM computer would be a flop, and Apple even ran a mocking full-page advertisement in the *Wall Street Journal* headlined, "Welcome, IBM. Seriously."

Behind the scenes, though, Steve Jobs, the head of Apple, knew that this new PC was a real threat to the Apple computer. The Apple was a favorite among those who owned it, but it was now likely to be underpriced by the newcomer. Jobs needed to move in a new direction, and that direction took him to Bellevue, Washington. Two weeks after the IBM PC launch, he arranged an urgent meeting with Bill Gates.

LIFE AT MICROSOFT

Microsoft began the 1980s in a healthy financial position. Sales each year were worth millions, and the company had no debts, unlike even some very successful companies. New orders for more software were flowing in at an amazing rate. In addition, bright people like Charles Simonyi kept knocking on Gates's door, looking for work.

KEEPING UP WITH THE GROWTH

Despite this flow of eager new employees, Gates recognized that Microsoft was in danger of falling behind in its many contracts if it did not hire more people. He asked Ballmer and Simonyi to go on a **recruitment** drive among leading U.S. universities in an effort to attract even more new workers.

What Gates and his team offered was not the chance of an instant fortune, but the opportunity to work among other highly intelligent people with the same interests. Fourteen-hour days and seven-day weeks were common, they told potential employees, and

Bill Gates has always expected hard work and commitment from Mircrosoft's employees.

still young computer **programmers** jumped at the chance to join Gates and his team.

ANOTHER MOVE

All of these newly hired employees needed space to work, and the existing office space was becoming cramped. In November 1981, three weeks after taking on its hundredth employee, the Microsoft offices moved a mile north to a new building on Northup Way, Bellevue, Washington.

Gates was anxious to maintain the Microsoft traditions that had developed by that stage. Soft drinks remained free for all employees, everyone had a separate office with a window, and employees could communicate with each other by using **e-mail**.

The core partnership

Even though Microsoft was growing rapidly and taking on a wider range of products, the core of the company remained the two partners who founded it: Bill Gates and Paul Allen. People saw Allen as a creative "ideas man," while logical Gates would take those ideas and turn them into top-selling products. This lucky balance was also reflected in their personalities: Allen was laid-back and approachable, but Gates was intense and likely to shout if things were not going his way.

Billionaire Bill

Gates knew that his deep involvement with the IBM PC gave him the chance to boost Microsoft to world dominance. Others in the industry seemed to sense the same thing, and they began to view Microsoft in a new light.

The worm turns with Apple

Steve Jobs of the Apple Corporation was one of those who could sense Microsoft's new position. When he visited Microsoft after the IBM PC launch in 1981, he knew that the new computer that Apple was developing, the Apple Macintosh, would never succeed without Microsoft's involvement in the development.

In January 1982, Apple signed a deal with Microsoft to work together on developing the Apple Mac. Jobs was worried that Gates might use some of the features of the Mac, such as the mouse, in developing software for rivals, so he insisted that Microsoft could not use such features until January 1, 1983. That was the date that Apple had set for the launch of the Apple Mac.

Opening Windows

There was no way that the Apple Mac would be ready on time. Gates could see that it would take longer than Jobs had estimated to develop all the

> Bill is just the same as everyone else There
> are probably more smart people per square
> foot right here than anywhere else in the
> world, but Bill is just smarter.
>
> Mike Maples, Microsoft Executive
> Vice-President

different software elements involved. He was free
to go ahead with software as soon as the deadline
passed. He sent Microsoft into a frenzied push to
produce Windows, a computer **operating system**
that arranges data in a **Graphical User Interface**.
This system would match nearly anything that the
user–friendly Mac could do.

If Gates could establish Windows as the industry
standard, then any other company designing software
would have to design it to use on Windows.
Microsoft would rake in the money.

Windows was launched in November 1983 at the
Fall Comdex '83, an annual computer convention.
Banners and signs everywhere around the Las Vegas
convention center trumpeted the new arrival. The
Apple Mac was not launched until January 22, 1984.

INSTANT RECOGNITION

The Windows launch was a triumph, and sales
increased at an amazing rate. Gates, now seen as a

Master Of the Universe

Having conquered the world's computers, BILL GATES takes aim at banks, phone companies, even Hollywood. He's in for the fight of his life.

Time magazine's April 1984 cover headline echoed the public view of Bill Gates.

whiz kid or even a genius, was featured in dozens of magazine articles and even appeared on the cover of *Time* magazine in April 1984. Success followed success, and the next two years saw the final stage of Microsoft's move to computer software dominance.

At Gates's 30th birthday party in October 1985, guests were asked to dress on the theme of *The Great Gatsby*, the novel by F. Scott Fitzgerald. In the novel, Gatsby is a millionaire who throws lavish parties but is ultimately a mystery.

STOCK MARKET GOLD MINE

Microsoft decided to go public, to sell **shares** in the company, in early 1986. Going public indicates how well potential buyers think a company is performing. When many people want to buy, thinking that the company will do well, the share price increases.

Microsoft went public on March 13, 1986, and the public bought shares enthusiastically. By the end of the first day's trading, Gates had sold enough shares to earn a quick $1.7 million. Yet he still had a 45 percent share in Microsoft, with shares worth more than $3,000 million. Bill Gates was a billionaire.

End of an era

One of the biggest bombshells for Bill Gates and Microsoft came in March 1983, when Paul Allen left the company as a full-time employee because of health reasons. He had developed Hodgkin's Disease, a type of treatable cancer that drains a person's energy. This made Gates reconsider his own health and the punishing work schedule he imposed on his body. Paul Allen is better now and back on the board of Microsoft. He has put his money toward helping organizations that aim to widen the use of computers and **Internet** capability.

With the growing success of Microsoft, Gates was able to follow some interests outside work. He went out with women he met at computer gatherings. One woman in particular, Ann Winblad, revived his interest in movies and introduced him to new types of food, such as Thai cooking. This was a change from Gates's normal diet of fast food.

Frantic trading at the New York Stock Exchange on March 13, 1986, made Gates into a Billionaire.

A WAVE OF TRIUMPHS

"More" seems to be the best word to describe the world of Gates and Microsoft from 1986 on. There were more contracts, each worth more money, needing more employees to finish on time so that Microsoft could attract even more business. All these employees, numbering 1,200 by that stage, needed more space. So in February 1986, Microsoft moved its headquarters to Redmond, Washington.

REFLECTING BILL'S VISION

The new offices, occupying 400 acres of Evergreen Place, reflected Gates's vision of the ideal working environment. There were four X-shaped buildings, none more than two stories high, and each dotted with many windows. As before, everyone had a separate office, and soft drinks remained free. In keeping with Gates's views of hard work, eating areas

Windows, already a Microsoft buzz word, looked out on bright courtyards at the new Redmond headquarters.

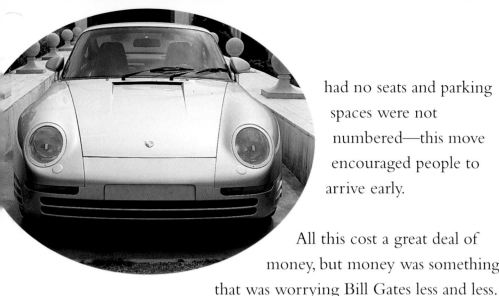

had no seats and parking spaces were not numbered—this move encouraged people to arrive early.

All this cost a great deal of money, but money was something that was worrying Bill Gates less and less.

Bill Gates satisfied his craving for speed in his Porsche 930 Turbo.

GENEROUS GESTURES

Gates was beginning to find other ways to spend some of his increasing fortune. In August 1986, he and Paul Allen donated $2.2 million to Lakeside School for a new mathematics and science building to be called Allen-Gates Hall. There was also a new outside interest in Gates's life—**biotechnology**. Gates began reading about this subject on a 1987 trip to Brazil, and the subject has remained a passionate interest for him. In 1991 he donated $12 million to the University of Washington. The money was to set up a new Department of Molecular Biology.

No LETTING UP

This new interest did not prove to be a distraction from Gates's main interest in life: computers and how they can be improved.

What's in a name?

Allen-Gates Hall, the new mathematics and science building at Lakeside School, could easily have been named Gates-Allen Hall. The matter was decided by the two friends with the flip of a coin. Gates guessed wrong, one of his few mistaken predictions.

He was eager to maintain his image as whiz kid **programmer,** even though he had to spend much of his time making important decisions about the future of Microsoft.

In May 1990, Gates led a team of West Coast computer experts across the country to Boston to take on an equivalent group of East Coast experts. They were competing in the light-hearted Computer Bowl, a contest about computer knowledge. Gates, who answered nearly all of his questions correctly, led the West to a narrow 300–290 point victory.

> You get Bill Gates in a room with his peers, and he will know more than anybody else in the room.
> J. Allen Grayson, who has worked with Gates for more than ten years *Time* magazine, 1995

Just two weeks later, Gates had another victory, with the launch of Windows 3.0, the latest version of Microsoft's money-spinning product. Taking over the conference room of an elegant New York hotel for the occasion, Microsoft also beamed a broadcast of the launch by satellite to Boston, Chicago, and other cities. Gates led the festivities and wound up a circus like performance by having a group of high-level computer experts add their praise to the new Windows product.

STILL GROWING

Shares in Microsoft continued to go up, increasing Gates's fortune even further. In April 1991, *Forbes* business magazine had the headline "Can Anyone Stop Him?" above a story on Gates. By early 1992, the rising value of Microsoft shares put Gates's fortune at more than $7 billion, making him the richest person in the United States.

Were there any new challenges left for Gates?

Microgames

Bill Gates's own family had always loved playing games, and eventually this interest found its way into the Microsoft way of life. Each summer Bill's parents would invite a number of Microsoft employees and other guests to a lakefront competition known as the Microgames. Guests would divide into teams and compete in a series of contests that involved problem solving, swimming, singing, and some sort of treasure hunt.

WINDOWS TO THE FUTURE

" **C**an Anyone Stop Him?" the magazine headline about Bill Gates seemed to sum up the feelings of many people about Microsoft and its influential chairperson. The Apple Corporation tried to do just that, with a **lawsuit** about the way in which Microsoft Windows used elements that could have been taken from the Apple Mac. That legal action failed in April 1992, but each side made various legal moves for a new trial, and the **verdict** a year later favored Microsoft.

THE HOME FRONT

Microsoft became the world's largest computer-industry company in January 1993 on the basis of the total value of its shares. Bill Gates was probably America's most eligible bachelor. But behind the scenes, he was becoming involved with Melinda French, one of Microsoft's marketing managers. On January 1, 1994, the two were married on the

Gate's lakefront house combines traditional wood construction with a high tech core using Microsoft software.

Hawaiian island of Lanai. Steve Ballmer was Gates's best man.

At the same time, work was in progress on Bill's new house, a series of five large pavilions set on the wooded banks of a lake shore not far from Microsoft headquarters. Many of Gates's own ideas had gone into the design of the house, including a huge **database** which would provide wall images of famous paintings and photographs for Gates and his guests.

SPREADING THE NET

Gates and Microsoft still had new areas to explore. Microsoft began widening its choice of **multimedia** software, including a successful range of **CD–ROMs**. Gates also looked for ways to use his own house ideas, such as the image databank, as profit-making business ideas. In 1995 he pumped millions of Microsoft dollars into DreamWorks SKG, the new movies, television, and music **studio** co-founded by Hollywood director Steven Spielberg.

WINDOWS 95

On August 24, 1995, Microsoft launched Windows 95, its most ambitious software package up to that date. Gates described it as an "operating environment," able to link and monitor the dozens of software applications that a computer might be running, even at the same time.

The figure of Bill Gates loomed over the long-awaited launch of Microsoft's Windows 95.

Some people had doubts about Windows 95. They said that its launch was delayed and even then, it was released with some problems. But by that time Microsoft's position was almost impossible to attack, and these criticisms never became a serious problem.

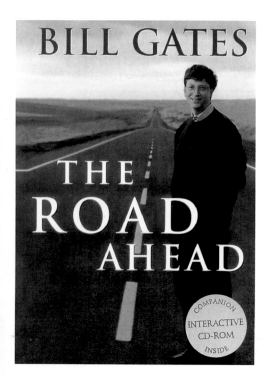

THE ROAD AHEAD

In 1996 Bill Gates published *The Road Ahead*, his personal vision of the future and how we will all live with increasingly advanced computers. The book was a worldwide best seller, showing the public's fascination with Microsoft's co founder.

Gates's own road took a new turn on April 26, 1996, when his wife Melinda gave birth to a daughter, Jennifer Katharine Gates.

Home from home?

Late 1997 brought news that Bill Gates was planning to spend more than $13 million on a mansion in one of the most fashionable areas of London. Like Gates's new home in the United States, the house would be equipped with a wide range of electronic gadgets. This showed a new interest in foreign countries, and Britain in particular, where Microsoft was investing $80 million in its largest research center outside of Seattle.

Bill Gates has helped shape the way in which we live today, and looks to the future with confidence.

As the 1990s draw to a close, Gates is determined to steer Microsoft into new directions, and in particular to benefit from the increased use of the **Internet** by businesses and individuals. There are obstacles standing in the way, but Gates is no stranger to setbacks and ultimate victory.

When you're lucky and successful, it's important not to get complacent. Luck can turn sour, and customers demand a lot of the people and companies they make successful. Big mistakes are rarely tolerated. I hope to remain successful but there are no guarantees.

Bill Gates, 1997

A VIEW ON GATES?

By the end of 1997, Bill Gates was believed to be the richest person in the world, with his Microsoft **shares** alone worth nearly $40 billion. Sometimes he would be listed as the second richest, after the oil-rich Sultan of Brunei, but this does not take into account the many investments that Gates holds in addition to his Microsoft shares.

FASCINATION WITH WEALTH

Some people are fascinated by Bill Gates because he has built a company from a room in an Albuquerque apartment building, and now he dominates the world of computers. The dozens of articles and interviews with Gates in the world's press show this wide interest.

> I was fortunate to have family and teachers who encouraged me. Children often thrive when they get that kind of attention.
>
> Bill Gates

But to many people, what makes Gates so interesting is his money. His fortune is hard to imagine and makes people wonder how they would spend it. Simply looking for information on the name "Bill Gates" on Internet uncovers hundreds of **web sites** devoted to everything about the man. One of these sites is devoted simply to the Gates fortune, and Internet users can check on how the Gates fortune has risen in a given day, or even minute.

HIGH-LEVEL RECOGNITION

The Bill Gates phenomenon has not been lost on government leaders around the world. In June 1992, U.S. President George Bush awarded Gates the National Medal of Technology to show how much Gates had transformed a whole industry with his vision and ideas. His position at the top of the computer world gives him the money and power to act on his ideas.

In addition to supporting many established charities dealing with social problems and the environment, Gates has added his own voice to shaping the future.

World leaders, such as Prime Minister Tony Blair of England and President Bill Clinton have called on Gates's knowledge and vision for the future.

Bill Gates has played a personal role in widening access to computers and to the Internet.

In June 1997, he and his wife established the Gates Library Foundation. The goal of this organization is to bring computer and Internet access to public libraries across the United States and Canada, especially in poorer areas. Gates has supported a similar plan by U.K. Prime Minister Tony Blair to link British schools with the Internet.

> From a personal standpoint, I've made my share of mistakes but there aren't many that I'd go back and change. Most mistakes in life wake us up to our limitations. They usually end up being some of the most valuable things we go through.   Bill Gates, 1997

A LESSON FOR OTHERS?

Bill Gates has taken risks throughout his life and has usually benefited from these decisions. By missing classes at school and later dropping out of college he devoted himself to computer programming. In doing so, he established his strong position just as the computer industry was beginning to skyrocket.

Later decisions, such as the move to devote all of Microsoft's staff, money, and time to developing Windows, provided similarly good results. But even Gates himself would discourage young people now from gambling too much with their education. True, he did take those risks, but in the end it was the hard work that translated those risks into his fortune and success.

Is Bill innovative? Yes. Does he appear innovative? No. Bill personally is a lot more innovative than Microsoft could ever be, simply because his way of doing business is to do it very steadfastly and very conservatively…. He lets things get out in the market and be tried first before he moves into them. And that's valid. It's like IBM.

Former Microsoft executive Alan Boyd comparing Gates with the [IBM] corporation that helped make his fortune

BILL GATES—TIMELINE

1955 Bill Gates born in Seattle, Washington (October 28)

1967 Enters Lakeside School

1968 First experience working on a computer, at Lakeside School

1969 Teams up with Paul Allen and other students to form Lakeside Programmers Group (LPG)

1971 Makes first deal, organizing LPG contract to write a payroll program for a local Seattle company

1972 Best friend Kent Evans dies in climbing accident

1973 Enters Harvard University

1974 Decides, with Paul Allen, to design a form of the **BASIC** computer **language** to sell to MITS for use in the Altair home-kit computer

1975 Deal arranged to supply BASIC to MITS. Microsoft formed in Albuquerque, New Mexico

1977 Drops out of Harvard to concentrate full time on Microsoft. Gains full control of Microsoft's version of BASIC from MITS

1979 Moves Microsoft headquarters to Seattle

1980 Signs deal with IBM to develop languages and **operating systems** for the new range of IBM **personal computers**. Acquires full ownership of DOS operating system, later to be the heart of all IBM computers

1981 Microsoft DOS (MS–DOS) introduced on all IBM computers

1982 Signs deal with Apple Computers to help develop software for new range of Macintosh computers

1983	Paul Allen leaves Microsoft because of ill health. Microsoft introduces WORD 1, its first applications program, and then Windows, a **Graphical User Interface**
1986	Microsoft launched on **stock** market, making Gates an instant billionaire. Allen and Gates donate $2.2 million to Lakeside School for new Mathematics and Science building
1990	Oversees launch of Microsoft Windows 3.0 to great success. Microsoft becomes first personal computer company to exceed $1 billion in sales in a single year
1992	Microsoft successfully turns aside Apple **lawsuit** claiming that Microsoft illegally used Apple ideas in its software. Gates honored by President George Bush with National Medal of Technology
1993	Microsoft becomes largest computer-related company in the world, based on the total value of its stock
1994	Marries Melinda French on the Hawaiian island of Lanai
1995	Windows 95, destined to become Microsoft's biggest ever seller, launched
1996	Daughter Jennifer Katharine Gates born (April 26)
1997	Establishes Gates Library Foundation, aiming to bring computer and **Internet** access to public libraries in the United States and Canada.

GLOSSARY

agent one who acts or has the power and authority to act on behalf of another

application special use for a computer or its software

BASIC acronym for Beginner's All-Purpose Symbolic Instruction Code, a computer **language** that new computer users can quickly learn and operate

biotechnology use of living organisms to produce drugs and other products that can help with medicine, recycling, pollution control, and manufacturing

book keeping recording the accounts and transactions of a business

CD–ROM compact disc on which a large amount of **data** is stored

commission fee, usually a percentage of the price, paid to a person or company when a product is sold

communist describes a type of political system in which nearly all power is held by the central government without individual freedoms

corporation way of organizing a company so that it can own land, and earn and spend money as if its members were one person

data the collection of information, such as facts, numbers, or codes that a computer can hold

database collection of **data** arranged for easy retrieval

e-mail short for electronic mail, the means of sending computer information to other computers using a **modem** link

executives managers or others in authority in a company

Graphical User Interface symbols that appear on a computer screen to show the kind of software it can run

Internet network of computers that use modems to link with each other on the World Wide Web

language set of characters, symbols, and rules to allow a computer to operate

lawsuit dispute that needs to be settled in a court of law

license charge a person or a company a fee for using software in their computer product

mainframe large computer which is often the core of a system serving many different users

microcomputer small computer with miniature elements to allow most computer functions

microprocessor tiny circuit that contains the information to operate a computer

minicomputer computer that can process more information than a personal computer but less than a mainframe

modem machine that links a computer to other computers somewhere else by using a telephone connection

mouse hand-operated device that directs the operations of a computer by pointing at different areas of the screen

multimedia computer products that include graphics, video, and sound

operating system collection of software that directs a computer's operations

personal computer microcomputer designed for individual use

prep school private school that prepares students for college

process perform operations on data

programmer someone who writes computer programs

recruitment seeking out new people, usually to join a company or other group

share one of the equal parts into which the overall value of a company has been divided

silicon chip tiny circuit that contains the information to operate a computer, made of silicon, a nonmetallic element; a microprocessor

Silicon Valley region in central Californian that has attracted a large number of computer-related companies

stock shares of a particular company or corporation

studio in cinema, a company that produces and distributes movies

subscribe pledge a sum of money as a payment

suburb district that is just outside a city, usually a smaller residential community

technology use of science for practical purposes

time sharing in computers, the paying of a fee to link up to a large central computer

user friendly in computers, the ease with which a product can be understood and used

verdict result of a court case

web site place on the Internet, where information about a particular subject is found

word processor computer that has all the features of a typewriter plus programs to correct or change text

World's Fair large fair featuring the accomplishments of individual countries or international companies

Index

Albuquerque 16, 18
Allen, Paul 10, 13, 14, 17, 27, 29, 35, 39
Allen-Gates Hall 41
Apple Computers 23, 33, 36-37, 44
Ballmer, Steve 15, 25, 29, 34, 45
Biotechnology 41
Blair, Tony 50
Bush, George 49
Computer Center Corporation ["Triple –C"] 12
DreamWorks SKG 45
Evans, Kent 13
Forbes magazine 43
Fortune magazine 29
French, Melinda 44
    Marries Bill Gates 45
Gates, Bill 4-5
    At Harvard University 15, 17
    At school 7-13
    Awarded National Medal of Technology 49
    Becomes a billionaire 39
    Childhood 6-9
    Estimated wealth 43, 48
    First business deal 13
    First experience with computers 11
    House 45
    Marriage and family 45-46
    Partnership with Allen 17, 27, 35
Gates, Jennifer [daughter] 46
Gates Library Foundation 50
Harvard University 15, 17
IBM 26-27, 30-33

Internet 47-48, 50
Jobs, Steve 22, 32, 33, 36
Lakeside Programmers Group 13-14
Lakeside School 10-13
Lubow, Miriam 20
McDonald, Marc 18
Microsoft 4-5
    Beginning of company 17
    Division of shares 29
    First million-dollar sales year 21
    Goes public 38-39
    Moves to Bellevue, Washington 21
    Moves to Redmond, Washington 40
MITS 16-19
Nippon Electric Company (NEC) 22-23, 27
Nishi, Kay 22-23
Perot, H. Ross 24-25
Sams, Jack 26
Seattle 6, 8
    World's Fair 7
Seattle Computer Products 27
Silicon Valley 20
Simonyi, Charles 28, 34
Spielberg, Steven 45
The Road Ahead [book] 46
Time magazine 38
Traf-O-Data 14-15
University of Washington 14, 41
Weiland, Ric 13, 18
Wimblad, Ann 39
Windows 37, 42, 51
Windows 95 46

More Books to Read

Dickinson, Joan D. *Bill Gates.* Springfield, NJ: Enslow Publishers, Inc. 1997.

Forman, Michael. *Bill Gates, Software Billionaire.* Morristown, NJ: Silver Burdett Press. 1998.

Simon, Charnan. Bill Gates. Danbury, CT: Children's Press. 1997.